THE OFFICIAL
007™
FACT FILE

JAMES BOND

Richard Holliss

·H·A·M·L·Y·N·

Published in 1989 by
The Hamlyn Publishing Group Limited
Michelin House, 81 Fulham Road, London SW3 6RB

ISBN 0 600 56320 0
Printed in Great Britain by Purnell Book Production Company Limited, Bristol.

This book deals with the James Bond 007 films, from *Dr No* onwards, made by Eon Productions Ltd. *Licence To Kill*
was made by Danjaq SA.

Acknowledgements
Front cover: Top and centre right © 1989 Danjaq S.A. and United Artists Company. All rights reserved. Centre left © 1971 Danjaq S.A. All rights reserved.
Bottom © 1985 Danjaq S.A. All rights reserved.
Back cover: Top left: 1974 Danjaq S.A. All rights reserved. Top right © 1977 Danjaq S.A. All rights reserved. Bottom © 1974 Danjaq S.A. All rights reserved.
Page 8: Top and centre © 1989 Danjaq S.A. and United Artists Company. All rights reserved. Bottom: © 1977 Danjaq S.A. All rights reserved.
Page 9: Top © 1967 Danjaq S.A. All rights reserved. Bottom © 1989 Danjaq S.A. and United Artists Company. All rights reserved.
Page 10: Top © 1989 Danjaq S.A. and United Artists Company. All rights reserved. Bottom © 1962 Danjaq S.A. All rights reserved.
Page 11: Top, bottom left and bottom right © 1989 Danjaq S.A. and United Artists Company. All rights reserved.
Page 12: © 1985 Danjaq S.A. All rights reserved.
Page 13: Top © 1971 Danjaq S.A. All rights reserved. Centre © 1974 Danjaq S.A. All rights reserved. Bottom © 1963 Danjaq S.A. All rights reserved.
Page 14: Top and bottom © 1962 Danjaq S.A. All rights reserved.
Page 15: Top, bottom left and bottom right © 1962 Danjaq S.A. All rights reserved.
Page 16: Top © 1962 Danjaq S.A. All rights reserved. Bottom © 1963 Danjaq S.A. All rights reserved.
Page 17: Top © 1965 Danjaq S.A. All rights reserved. Bottom: © 1964 Danjaq S.A. All rights reserved.
Page 18: Top © 1989 Danjaq S.A. and United Artists Company. All rights reserved. Bottom © 1965 Danjaq S.A. All rights reserved.
Page 19: Top left © 1963 Danjaq S.A. All rights reserved. Top right © 1985 Danjaq S.A. All rights reserved. Bottom © 1965 Danjaq S.A. All rights reserved.
Page 20: Top and bottom © 1964 Danjaq S.A. All rights reserved.
Page 21: Top and bottom © 1964 Danjaq S.A. All rights reserved.
Page 22: © 1962 Danjaq S.A. All rights reserved. © 1964 Danjaq S.A. All rights reserved. © 1974 Danjaq S.A. All rights reserved. © 1977 Danjaq S.A. All
rights reserved.
Page 23: © 1983 Danjaq S.A. All rights reserved.
Page 24: Top and bottom © 1964 Danjaq S.A. All rights reserved.
Page 25: Top and bottom © 1964 Danjaq S.A. All rights reserved.
Page 26: Top and bottom © 1977 Danjaq S.A. All rights reserved.
Page 27: Top and bottom © 1987 Danjaq S.A. and United Artists Company. All rights reserved.
Page 28: Top and bottom © 1977 Danjaq S.A. All rights reserved.
Page 29: Top and bottom © 1977 Danjaq S.A. All rights reserved.
Page 30: Top © 1967 Danjaq S.A. All rights reserved. Bottom © 1971 Danjaq S.A. All rights reserved.
Page 31: Top and bottom © 1973 Danjaq S.A. All rights reserved.
Page 32: Top © 1977 Danjaq S.A. All rights reserved. Bottom © 1983 Danjaq S.A. All rights reserved.
Page 33: Top and centre © 1967 Danjaq S.A. All rights reserved. Bottom © 1979 Danjaq S.A. All rights reserved.
Page 36: Left © 1967 Danjaq S.A. All rights reserved. Right © 1971 Danjaq S.A. All rights reserved.
Page 37: Top and bottom © 1977 Danjaq S.A. All rights reserved. Centre © 1974 Danjaq S.A. All rights reserved.
Page 38: Top © 1979 Danjaq S.A. All rights reserved. Centre: © 1985 Danjaq S.A. All rights reserved. Bottom © 1987 Danjaq S.A. and United Artists
Company. All rights reserved.
Page 39: Top © 1964 Danjaq S.A. All rights reserved. Centre © 1977 Danjaq S.A. All rights reserved. Bottom © 1973 Danjaq S.A. All rights reserved.
Page 40: Top and bottom © 1979 Danjaq S.A. All rights reserved.
Page 41: Top and bottom © 1979 Danjaq S.A. All rights reserved.
Page 42: Top and bottom © 1974 Danjaq S.A. All rights reserved.
Page 43: © 1977 Danjaq S.A. All rights reserved.
Page 44: Top and bottom © 1983 Danjaq S.A. All rights reserved.
Page 45: Top left, top right and bottom © 1983 Danjaq S.A. All rights reserved.
Pages 46-47: Top © 1985 Danjaq S.A. All rights reserved. Centre © 1974 Danjaq S.A. All rights reserved. Bottom © 1973 Danjaq S.A. All rights reserved.
Page 48: © 1987 Danjaq S.A. and United Artists Company. All rights reserved.
Page 49: Top © 1977 Danjaq S.A. All rights reserved. Bottom © 1971 Danjaq S.A. All rights reserved.
Page 50: Top and bottom © 1987 Danjaq S.A. and United Artists Company. All rights reserved.
Page 51: Top, centre and bottom © 1987 Danjaq S.A. and United Artists Company. All rights reserved.
Page 52: Top © 1964 Danjaq S.A. All rights reserved. Bottom © 1987 Danjaq S.A. and United Artists Company. All rights reserved.
Page 53: Top © 1977 Danjaq S.A. All rights reserved. Bottom © 1969 Danjaq S.A. All rights reserved.
Page 54: Top and bottom © 1985 Danjaq S.A. All rights reserved.
Page 55: Top and bottom © 1989 Danjaq S.A. and United Artists Company. All rights reserved.
Page 56: © 1989 Danjaq S.A. and United Artists Company. All rights reserved.
Page 57: Top, bottom left and bottom right © 1989 Danjaq S.A. and United Artists Company. All rights reserved.
Page 58: Top and bottom © 1989 Danjaq S.A. and United Artists Company. All rights reserved.
Page 59: Top, centre and bottom © 1989 Danjaq S.A. and United Artists Company. All rights reserved.
Page 60: Top © 1979 Danjaq S.A. All rights reserved. Bottom © 1971 Danjaq S.A. All rights reserved.
Page 61: © 1974 Danjaq S.A. All rights reserved.

CONTENTS

WHAT MAKES A TOP SECRET AGENT?

Taking risks is an everyday part of being a top agent. In Licence To Kill *Bond lowers himself from the wing of a plane on to a moving tanker in a bid to capture the drugs baron, Sanchez.*

PELIGRO   INFLAMABLE

What makes a top secret agent like James Bond? For, in many respects, he is a superman. To survive all manner of awesome ordeals and ruthless enemies, he must be a highly trained professional. Adept at handling himself in dangerous situations, his assignments call for great courage and tenacity.

A martial arts expert, Bond needs super-strength and cunning to defeat his adversaries, but being a secret agent requires other important skills such as being able to pilot an aircraft, or steer a high-speed boat. Fearless and determined, these exceptional

Penetrating enemy territory is sometimes safer underwater to avoid detection by armed guards.

James Bond's assignments take him to some exotic locations. Here he visits an old friend in Egypt while trying to recover stolen microfilm in The Spy Who Loved Me.

qualities are the only protection that he might have in a life-or-death escape. A secret agent needs an extensive knowledge of his organization's foreign network, so that contacts working in the field can be easily located for all leads to an enemy's whereabouts. He must also be able to operate undercover and keep secret his true identity.

Posing as a marine specialist called Robert Sterling, Bond infiltrated Karl Stromberg's ocean fortress Atlantis and, in order to avoid detection, was briefed so that he could answer any difficult questions his host might ask in order to avoid detection. A master professional, Bond has even surprised his own superiors by revealing a more than thorough knowledge of an assignment. Q of the special weapons division was amazed at 007's expertise when discussing the origin of a rare orchid – the plant used to produce a deadly nerve gas which was at the centre of billionaire Hugo Drax's plan to destroy mankind.

Disguises are a vital part of an agent's undercover work. Here Bond is the groom in a fake Japanese marriage ceremony from You Only Live Twice.

A former naval commander, James Bond is still entitled to use the rank. This proved particularly helpful when he led the American forces against the crew of the tanker *Liparus,* after it hijacked three nuclear submarines. Normally, however, he introduces himself with "My name is Bond, James Bond." To the British Secret Service he is known as 007, the 00 prefix meaning that he is an agent with a licence to kill. On the rare occasion Bond is not pitting his wits against some evil foe, he lives quietly in an elegant London flat. Well dressed and sophisticated, Bond enjoys the company of beautiful women, a number of whom he has met on various assignments around the world. His favourite drink is dry Martini, "shaken but not stirred", yet if the occasion requires champagne then only Bollinger will do.

Bond and his handgun make a deadly team.

9

WHAT MAKES A TOP SECRET AGENT?

On several assignments 007 has needed the help of his old friend and CIA agent Felix Leiter. In the latest film, Bond is the best man at Leiter's wedding.

Wearing the right clothes on a mission is very important. Fortunately Q has ensured that 007 possesses an extensive wardrobe, whether it be the necessary outfit for underwater swimming, scaling a steep rockface or surviving the freezing cold of some mountainous region. When a crime syndicate was flooding the British and United States markets with illicit goods, Bond had to swim underwater to their hideout and destroy it with an explosive charge. He wore a watertight frogman's wet suit over the top of an immaculate tuxedo, so he could then assume the identity of an innocent passer-by.

As well as the incredible secret weapons that Q gives Bond at the start of an assignment, 007 never travels without his personal handgun – a Walther PPK 7.65mm automatic with a silencer attachment.

Among the most formidable of James Bond's adversaries have been the ruthless masterminds, determined upon world

Even when relaxing, Bond enjoys taking a risk.

domination. Most worked independently of each other and were financed in their warped projects by personal fortunes. To stop them, 007 has needed to understand every facet of their organizations and how they manipulated power to their own ends. Destroying the enemies' installations and bringing the villains to justice is Bond's top priority.

There have been, unfortunately, others – namely Dr No and Emilio Largo – dedicated to an even greater, more sinister leader. Their boss was the devious Ernst Stavro Blofeld and his organization SPECTRE (Special Executive for Counter Intelligence, Terrorism, Revenge and Extortion) was only prevented from achieving its evil aims by Bond's timely intervention.

Bond is always able to defend himself whenever the need arises.

Bond had a number of reasons for hating Blofeld. One was the death of his wife, Teresa, Contessa di Vicenzo. 007's happiness was cut short when she was murdered on their honeymoon by Blofeld. The villain had shot at Bond but missed; instead the bullet had killed Teresa – or Tracy as everyone knew her.

In James Bond's latest assignment, he accompanies his friend Felix Leiter of the CIA on a mission to capture a particularly vicious criminal, a billionaire drug baron called Sanchez. Fraught with danger, the task requires all Bond's skills and cunning so that he can first befriend and then capture the villain. It is just another example of the hard work and outstanding qualities that make 007 the British Secret Service's best and most successful agent.

In the latest film, Bond is helped by the beautiful Pam Bouvier.

An agent needs all his ingenuity and cunning to escape capture.

INSIDE THE

SECRET SERVICE

The success of any mission relies not only on the skill of agents like James Bond, but also on a well-briefed and efficient organization to back them up. M runs one such team of highly trained people at a secret headquarters in London. It is here that contact is made with foreign governments, politicians and even the Prime Minister. After processing any classified documents vital to British security and world peace, it is M's job to select the agent he thinks will be best suited to carry out the task in hand.

To protect his cover, M's real name is known only to a few privileged top-ranking officials. A strict disciplinarian, he shows a stern devotion to duty and tends to frown on 007's seemingly frivolous attitude towards a dangerous assignment. But, secretly, M has great admiration and respect for Bond and knows only too well what an outstanding agent he is.

Although M's offices are located in central London, they are expertly concealed from prying eyes. No one outside the organization even suspects that this calm and fatherly figure is, in fact, in charge of a network of agents around the world.

Miss Moneypenny is M's personal secretary. Situated in an outer office, she is always on hand to transmit valuable information from her boss to agents on assignment. Miss Moneypenny has a deep affection for James Bond and is always concerned when the Secret Service loses contact with him in a foreign territory.

Miss Moneypenny must also be prepared to accompany M to an overseas rendezvous if the need arises. During one such mission in which 007 was investigating a plot to upset world peace, M and his dedicated secretary had to take up residence in a temporary headquarters beneath an Egyptian temple in Cairo.

Miss Moneypenny, M's loyal personal assistant. 007 is her favourite agent.

Bond shares a joke with Miss Moneypenny in From Russia With Love.

Q proudly displays one of his department's amazing secret weapons in Diamonds Are Forever.

M occasionally seeks James Bond's advice on the best way of dealing with a difficult assignment as seen here in The Man With The Golden Gun.

Among Bond's other contacts at headquarters is Major Boothroyd, the brilliant inventor of special equipment vital to the success of any mission. Known throughout the Secret Service by the codename of Q, his ingenious secret weapons could mean the difference between life and death for Bond. These devices come in all shapes and sizes, from a dart-firing wristwatch to a sleek Aston Martin with more hidden weaponry than a tank.

Although not a member of the British Secret Service but of the CIA, agent Felix Leiter is a valuable member of Bond's team. He first appeared in 007's brush with Dr No and returned on numerous occasions to help Bond overthrow such dangerous masterminds as Goldfinger, Emilio Largo, Dr Kananga and General Koskov. In the latest adventure, Leiter is working for the Drug Enforcement Administration. He teams up with Bond to capture the evil Sanchez but this has dreadful consequences for the courageous American.

13

Dr No, the evil genius behind the missile "toppling" device.

DR. NO

When communication is severed between London and Jamaica, M assigns James Bond to find out what has happened to British Secret Service agent Strangways and his secretary. Arriving in Kingston, clues to Strangways' disappearance lead 007 to the mysterious and unhelpful Professor Dent. Later that day Bond meets boat-owner Quarrel and Felix Leiter.

Leiter explains Cape Canaveral's concern that radio interference from the Jamaica area will affect their next moon launch. Most of the interference is coming from an isolated peninsula called Crab Key, steeped in legends of fire-breathing dragons. Unbeknown to Bond, however, Professor Dent travels to Crab Key for fresh instructions on how to dispose of him, from the fiendish scientist Dr No. Later that evening Bond narrowly escapes being bitten by a poisonous tarantula placed in his hotel room.

In the morning, 007 visits Government House in search of files on Dr No and the mysterious Crab Key, though is not surprised to learn that they have vanished. The treacherous secretary, Miss Taro, lures Bond to her cottage. But Bond, realizing it is a trap, arranges to have the girl arrested. When Professor Dent arrives to kill Bond, he is interrogated by 007, who is forced to shoot him in self-defence.

The legendary "dragon" of Crab Key is not what it seems.

Bond, Quarrel and Honey Ryder explore Dr No's island paradise.

penetration of the Superpowers' rocket systems is just the first step.

Bond is imprisoned, but manages to escape through a ventilation shaft in his cell. Stealing a radiation suit, he infiltrates Dr No's secret laboratory. With seconds to spare before the launch from Cape Canaveral, 007 sabotages the missile "toppling" device by overloading the nuclear reactor. As the base is evacuated, the evil doctor tries to kill Bond, but perishes when he falls into the boiling "heavy" water surrounding the nuclear core.

Bond rescues Honey from drowning and in the resulting pandemonium the two escape in a stolen motor launch as Dr No's base is obliterated by a gigantic explosion. Adrift at sea, Bond and Honey are eventually picked up by Felix Leiter's patrol boat.

On discovering that geological samples collected from Crab Key, by Strangways, are radioactive and with only 48 hours before the next moon shot, Bond sets off for Crab Key with Quarrel as a guide. In the morning Bond meets up with Honey Ryder, a beautiful girl who collects seashells to sell at the market. When a gunboat damages her canoe, Honey has no option but to accompany Bond and Quarrel inland. Pursued by Dr No's guards, the three meet up with the legendary "fire-breathing" dragon.

Quarrel is incinerated and Bond and Honey are captured by the occupants of the "monster", which turns out to be a cleverly disguised tank.

They are taken to Dr No's headquarters, where the sinister member of SPECTRE outlines to Bond his plan of world domination, of which the

Bond meets Honey Ryder on the beach at Crab Key.

Bond dispatches one of Dr No's henchmen.

15

VILLAINS' GALLERY
(Part One)

ROSA KLEBB

A mission to retrieve a valuable cypher machine took 007 to Istanbul. It is there that he came face to face with the vicious Rosa Klebb. An evil and tyrannical woman, Klebb began her career as head of operations for SMERSH, the organization for Soviet Counter-intelligence. Although remaining in the background to co-ordinate and train SPECTRE agents for vital sabotage missions, Klebb was forced to confront Bond in person when her plans to kill him ended in failure. With deadly determination she attempted to eliminate 007 by kicking him to death with poisonous blades concealed in the front of her shoes.

RED GRANT

Istanbul was also the destination of another of James Bond's most dangerous opponents, Klebb's trained killer and SPECTRE hit man, Red Grant. A convicted murderer, Grant escaped from jail and was given sanctuary by SPECTRE. Biding his time before carrying out his orders, Grant actually protected Bond by eliminating various SMERSH agents.

Once the valuable cypher machine was safely delivered from the Russians' hands into those of the sinister Blofeld and SPECTRE, Grant's care for 007 took on a whole new meaning. In a cramped compartment aboard the Istanbul Express, Bond finally met up with his would-be assassin. A brutal fight followed. Fortunately, 007 was the victor.

Dr No, SPECTRE's key agent who appropriated international funds for his own devious ends. See full story on page 14.

See full story on page 14.

SPECTRE agent Red Grant doesn't even flinch when Rosa Klebb punches him in the stomach in From Russia With Love.

EMILIO LARGO

With agents like James Bond continually thwarting SPECTRE's criminal activities, the organization's funding was at an all time low. After dedicated villains like Dr No, Rosa Klebb and Red Grant were safely disposed of, SPECTRE's new number 2, Emilio Largo, then hit upon an ingenious plan for making money.

He successfully hijacked and sank a Vulcan bomber containing two atomic warheads and then held the British Government to ransom for £100 million in uncut diamonds. M gave Bond just two days to infiltrate and destroy Largo's headquarters in the Bahamas before the explosive deadline, when Largo threatened to detonate the bomb in a British or American city.

An evil, deadly genius, Largo enjoyed throwing his enemies to the man-eating sharks he kept in his swimming-pool. A millionaire through his criminal connections, Largo also owned a sophisticated yacht called the *Disco Volante* which served as the base for his underwater operations, such as salvaging the atomic devices from the sunken bomber.

The yacht was also designed to divide, so the front half became a hydrofoil with a top speed of 150 km/h (95mph) and the back, a fully armed battleship used by Largo to repel any pursuing gunboat.

Fortunately, like his ill-fated colleagues before him, Largo reckoned without the intervention of James Bond.

Emilio Largo, the mastermind in charge of restoring SPECTRE's ailing funds from Thunderball.

Auric Goldfinger, whose lust for wealth nearly destroyed the US gold reserve at Fort Knox. See full story on page 20.

Q'S INVENTIONS

Head of the British Secret Service's special armaments division is Major Boothroyd or Q as he is better known. Slightly eccentric, he is the ingenious designer of a wonderful array of gadgets and vehicles necessary to help agents like 007 accomplish any vital mission. When Bond set off alone to track down an evil drugs baron, Q disobeyed orders and travelled out to Isthmus City in Central America to assist with a bag of lethal MI6 tricks.

Q shows Bond his latest invention: an innocent-looking camera that converts into a lethal signature gun from Licence To Kill.

At Q's secret headquarters, Bond is often witness to some of the incredible inventions being tested for use in the field. For example, parking meters that eject a cloud of gas, a steel-edged tea tray that travels at high speed over a cushion of air to deal any enemy a deadly blow, a machine-gun post hidden within the dummy of a Mexican figure, a lethal umbrella that snaps shut around the victim's head when it rains and an exploding portable cassette player which Q affectionately refers to as a "ghetto blaster".

Other sophisticated aids to spying include a photocopier hidden in a cigarette case, a signet ring that takes photographs, a wallet-sized device that can assist the opening of a safe by showing an X-ray image of the lock mechanism, a watch with a hyper-intensive magnetic field powerful enough to deflect bullets at close range and a 3-D visual identikit which accesses foreign police records in order to build up a picture of a particular suspect.

When Bond found himself at the mercy of Hugo Drax, the mastermind intent on destroying humanity, his unique wrist-watch that fired five armour-piercing bullets and five cyanide-coated darts came to the rescue. It also proved useful when Bond had to stop Drax's spaceflight-simulating centrifuge from crushing him.

Bond makes a successful lift-off with the help of his own personal jet-pack from Thunderball.

Tatiana Romanova reveals her love for Bond, little realizing that he is taping everything she says with the aid of a rather special camera in From Russia With Love.

"Snooper", Q's sophisticated canine surveillance robot, is sent out by the British Secret Service to track down 007. Bond has mysteriously disappeared during an assignment to stop Max Zorin from destroying America's Silicon Valley in A View To A Kill.

Other unique and clever gadgets have included a four-minute breathing capsule, which Bond found extremely useful when investigating Emilio Largo's underwater operations, and a specially designed key-ring. This proved vital to the survival of Bond and Kara Milovy when they were imprisoned by communis police in Afghanistan. By whistling a personal code to the key-ring programmed by Q, it automatically ejects a stun gas pellet which overpowers the guard for five seconds – long enough for Bond to turn the tables on his adversaries.

Another of Q's versatile gadgets included what appeared to be, on the outside, an ordinary black leather case. However, its contents included ammunition, a knife-throwing device, a tear gas canister that explodes if the locks are forced and a folding sniper rifle. For the same mission, a miniature tape-recorder was concealed inside a normal twin-flex camera so Bond could tape the beautiful Tatiana's confessions aboard the Istanbul ferry.

With the aid of special breathing apparatus designed by Q, Bond avoids being detected by Emilio Largo's men in Thunderball.

GOLDFINGER

"I expect you to die!" the villainous Goldfinger tells an anxious James Bond as he watches the laser's lethal beam of light inch towards him.

In Miami, James Bond strikes up a friendship with the attractive Jill Masterson. Jill's jealous boss, known by the intriguing name of Auric Goldfinger, punishes his employee – he suffocates her by spraying her whole body with gold paint.

The British Government is concerned that Goldfinger is smuggling gold overseas, and so M assigns 007 to the case. Secret Service inventor Major Boothroyd (Q) supplies him with a specially converted Aston Martin DB5.

Bond meets Goldfinger at the millionaire's country club. Embittered by 007's success in a "friendly" game of golf, Goldfinger warns him against any further involvement in his affairs by requesting his man-servant, a Korean martial arts expert called Oddjob, to demonstrate the deadly accuracy of his remarkable steel-rimmed bowler hat.

Goldfinger's love for "all that glitters" proves to be fatal for his secretary Jill Masterson.

Goldfinger's plan to explode a nuclear bomb inside Fort Knox is interrupted by the arrival of the United States Army.

Bond confidently points out the logistics of such an undertaking: the fact that $15 billion in gold weighs 10,500 tonnes and that it would take 60 men 12 days to load the gold on to 200 trucks! But Goldfinger does not intend to steal the gold, instead he will detonate a cobalt iodine atomic device inside the vault to render the gold radioactive for up to 60 years. The authorities will be forced to buy his gold at ten times the price.

Escaping, Bond manages to persuade Pussy Galore to substitute a knock-out gas for the lethal chemical, and Marines arrive to stop Golfinger's men. Bond is handcuffed to the atomic bomb but breaks free in time to protect himself from the sinister Oddjob who has orders to kill him. Electrocuting his adversary, 007 watches as a bomb-disposal team arrives just in time to stop the deadly countdown.

Ignoring these threats, Bond follows Goldfinger to Switzerland where he discovers that the villain is illegally exporting 18-carat gold bars inside the framework of his Rolls Royce Phantom. When Bond tries to escape in his weapons-laden Aston Martin, he is overpowered and captured. Goldfinger delights in the possibility of cutting him in half with an industrial laser, but he changes his mind when 007 reveals that he overheard him discussing a secret assignment called "Operation Grandslam".

Imprisoning Bond at his ranch in Kentucky, Goldfinger boasts of his daring scheme to break into the American gold reserve at Fort Knox. "Man has achieved miracles in every field of human endeavour, except crime," he tells Bond. While a team of female pilots led by Pussy Galore sprays the area with lethal nerve gas to kill the 41,000 troops stationed around the vault, Goldfinger and his men will break in.

On a flight to Washington, to be congratulated by the President, Bond and Pussy Galore find themselves held at gunpoint by the demented Goldfinger. A stray bullet, however, pierces the window of the aircraft's pressurized cabin and the fanatical madman is sucked out. As the plane loses altitude, Bond and Pussy Galore parachute to safety.

Goldfinger's Korean man-servant, Oddjob, proves a worthy adversary for 007.

21

BOND QUIZ 1

Picture Puzzle

The photographs of five of Bond's enemies have been cut and jumbled up. Can you identify them?

WORD PUZZLE

Hidden in these jumbled letters are 34 characters who have appeared in James Bond films. The words may read forwards, backwards, up, down or diagonally, but always in a straight line. When you have found one of the names, draw a ring around the letters. The hidden people are listed below – finding Q or M doesn't count!

A	E	M	C	G	R	K	J	O	M	A	K	C	Y	U	H	M	N	K	Y	S
G	K	E	I	S	O	J	N	N	O	J	C	S	J	V	G	A	S	A	N	U
P	O	B	H	S	L	L	R	D	L	G	S	J	R	P	F	X	C	R	N	E
D	R	G	K	V	T	T	D	Q	H	U	J	S	X	V	A	Z	K	A	E	V
M	H	O	R	M	S	J	G	F	P	H	O	Y	C	R	J	O	P	M	P	X
R	V	W	U	K	O	I	I	O	I	N	I	Z	D	U	Y	R	E	I	Y	Z
K	A	L	Z	B	L	C	T	Z	B	N	T	O	S	R	L	I	L	L	E	W
I	N	K	B	L	E	C	Q	M	O	I	G	P	C	Q	N	N	L	O	N	C
D	A	W	L	E	O	F	Q	R	N	U	N	E	A	C	S	O	X	V	O	E
D	N	G	O	A	H	P	I	V	H	U	S	D	R	R	K	O	H	Y	M	D
R	Y	T	F	B	R	J	P	U	S	S	Y	G	A	L	O	R	E	T	N	M
E	A	A	E	R	K	G	S	M	X	U	L	L	M	D	M	B	L	O	J	E
D	A	S	L	E	L	W	O	I	M	R	O	S	A	K	L	E	B	B	V	C
Y	M	T	D	O	H	Q	L	R	C	E	C	C	N	H	H	S	I	Z	W	D
R	A	R	Q	O	P	E	R	E	S	D	Q	P	G	C	E	B	U	E	Y	F
Y	S	O	P	C	F	N	E	K	T	G	U	K	A	M	A	L	K	H	A	N
E	O	M	R	W	I	N	T	A	B	R	E	E	A	E	L	F	G	C	D	G
N	V	B	M	M	E	S	D	T	N	A	J	J	J	Z	C	Z	F	J	N	Y	H
O	A	E	V	F	E	L	S	I	B	N	I	C	K	N	A	C	K	A	A	W
H	L	R	C	R	P	W	C	H	X	T	Q	C	H	O	C	J	T	S	M	X
M	Q	G	K	S	W	A	J	W	P	I	U	A	G	N	A	N	A	K	R	D

Anya Amasova
Blofeld
Dr Kananga
Dr No
Felix
Gobinda
Goldfinger
Honey Ryder
Hugo Drax
James Bond
Jaws
Kamal Khan
Kara Milovy
Koskov
Krest
Largo
Locque
Max Zorin
May Day
Moneypenny
Mr Big
Mr Kidd
Mr Wint
Nick Nack
Octopussy
Oddjob
Pussy Galore
Rosa Klebb
Red Grant
Sanchez
Scaramanga
Stromberg
Tee Hee
Whitaker

In which film was Bond eaten by a crocodile?

DID YOU KNOW?

When the producers of *The Spy Who Loved Me* looked at the designs for the interior of the *Liparus* oil tanker, they realized that no studio in the world was big enough to house it. In the film, this enormous tanker held three captured nuclear submarines. Albert R. Broccoli decided to build his own studio on a stretch of open ground at Pinewood Studios, England. The world's largest film stage, the "007 Stage" as it was called, measured 102 metres (336 feet) in length by 49 metres (160 feet) wide. Its cavernous roof hung 16 metres (53 feet) above the ground.

Turn to page 61 for the answers

James Bond 007 confidently leans on the bonnet of his sophisticated and gadget-laden Aston Martin DB5 in Goldfinger.

James Bond's driving skills are tested to the limit when he has to escape from pursuing enemy agents. Fortunately Q, the British Secret Service's brilliant inventor, has seen to it that 007's personal transportation is more than a match for such a need.

Each car has been furnished with some amazing technological devices. Perhaps Q's most impressive accomplishment was the Aston Martin DB5. A fast and efficient car, Bond used it on two of his most perilous assignments. The first time was in his fight against Auric Goldfinger, who was determined to contaminate America's gold reserves, and then against Emilio Largo, who had stolen two British atomic bombs and was holding the government to ransom.

The car body and windows were designed to be bullet proof. In emergencies, a protective shield could be raised to cover the back window. At the flick of a switch, the front headlights folded away to reveal retractable machine-guns, each capable of firing at an enemy roadblock. A dummy exhaust-pipe doubled as the launch tube for a treacherous oil slick and smoke-screen to deter any following car. If, however, an enemy managed to pull alongside, as sniper Tilly Masterson did while Bond was trailing Goldfinger through the Swiss Alps, then rotating tyre slashers could be extended from the DB5's wheel hubs to shred instantly the assailant's car tyres.

To an onlooker, the Aston Martin's interior appeared innocent enough, but hidden below the driver's arm rest were the controls for the car's weapon systems. An ordinary-looking radio speaker housed a miniature radar screen so Bond could pin-point the location of an enemy vehicle some miles ahead.

The car's most formidable weapon was operated by pressing a red button housed in the flip top of the gear-stick. When one of Goldfinger's men climbs into the car next to Bond, he has no idea what is in store for him. As the car speeds back to the villain's headquarters, Bond waits for just the right moment. . .
The thug's trigger-finger tightens, then 007 presses the button. In a split-second his luckless passenger is catapulted through a cleverly concealed gap in the car roof by a powerful ejector seat. The Aston Martin was also fitted with revolving number plates to provide further confusion.

To help James Bond's investigations into the mysterious undersea kingdom of evil Karl Stromberg, Q recommended that 007 used a most unusual car for the mission, a white aerodynamically-designed Lotus Esprit.

A non-lethal accessory to the Aston Martin DB5, but a very important addition to its defences, is a revolving number plate to confuse Bond's enemies.

1. Browning machine-gun (·303) with special short barrel. Moves forward from behind sidelights
2. Radio telephone in secret door compartment
3. Secret drawer of guns: Smith and Wesson magnum ·357 revolver, Smith and Wesson Centennial ·38 combat special, 7·65-mm Mauser machine-pistol
4. Retractable tyre slasher (left and right side)
5. Smoke cartridge underneath
6. Ejector pipe for triple-spiked nails
7. Extending over-rider rams (front and back)
8. Rotating number plate unit
9. Hot oil ejector pipe (lights swing down)
10. Bullet-proof retractable shield
11. Ejector seat for unwelcome passengers
12. Control console
13. Ejector seat button under false gear lever knob
14. Radar screen for tracking the enemy
15. Radar scanning in mirror
16. Ammunition box

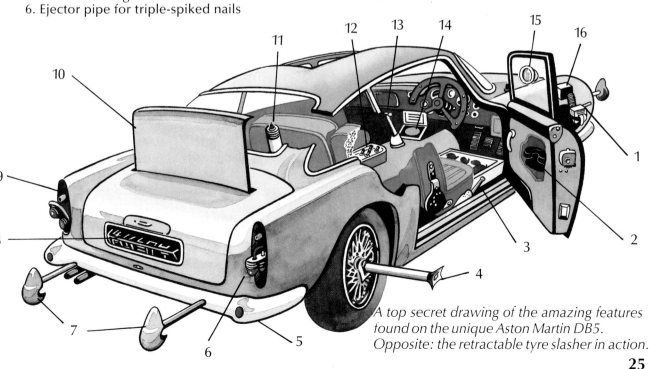

A top secret drawing of the amazing features found on the unique Aston Martin DB5. Opposite: the retractable tyre slasher in action.

In a death-defying chase, Bond is called upon to put the amazing Esprit through its paces. Accompanied by the beautiful Russian agent Major Anya Amasova, he first has to dodge an enemy motor-cyclist with a deadly missile disguised as a sidecar. The bullet-proof Lotus must then out-run and eventually destroy, with the aid of its secret weaponry, a car full of gun-toting assassins including the metal-toothed Jaws, by spraying a fine coat of paint on to the enemies' windscreen.

The amazing Lotus Esprit could travel just as easily underwater as on land.

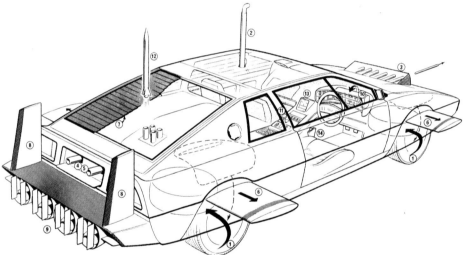

A plan of the attack and defence systems installed in James Bond's Lotus Esprit, which were put to the test in The Spy Who Loved Me.

1. Wheels turn and retract
2. Periscope
3. Harpoon guns
4. Cement guns
5. Oil release guns
6. Hydroplanes
7. Protective louvres
8. Rudder units
9. Propulsion units
10. Dashboard converts to underwater control panel
11. Missile firing control
12. Rocket missile
13. TV monitor
14. Submarine activator

But danger is never far away as Bond discovers when a helicopter piloted by Stromberg's assistant, Naomi, descends from the clouds, pitting the road with a hail of machine-gun fire. Bond is finally forced to drive off the end of a jetty into the sea. But the flick of a switch converts the Lotus into a submersible. Gliding peacefully below the waves, Bond detects the helicopter hovering above and launches a deadly missile. His airborne adversary explodes in a ball of orange flames.

When Bond decides to take a closer look at the sunken supports of Stromberg's home, the Lotus has to do battle with enemy submarines, before 007 can transform the strange underwater craft back into a car. The inhabitants of a crowded Sardinian beach look on in amazement as Bond drives straight out of the sea. Unfortunately the Lotus is destroyed on Bond's next assignment in a brush with the psychopathic Emile Locque's henchmen. Q immediately replaces it with a red-coloured model, but the mission requires none of its sophisticated weaponry.

The Volante's jet propulsion unit is powerful enough to catapult it through the air to safety.

When a plan is unearthed to assassinate secret service agents, Q supplies Bond with his latest design in personal transportation – the Aston Martin Volante. When Bond and Kara Milovy escape into the mountains of Czechoslovakia, the military police give chase. Bond slows them down by cutting through their car chassis with a high-intensity laser beam. Hastily blocking the road to the border with a large truck, the authorities watch helplessly as the Aston Martin fires a volley of rockets at the obstruction and completely destroys it.

Driving on to a frozen lake, the Volante skids to a halt when an enemy armoured car punctures one of its tyres. At the flick of a switch, two retractable skis are extended and with specially studded wheels the car is propelled across the ice at top speed by a rocket propulsion unit under the back bumper. Leaping above the heads of the astonished military, the car lands in a snowdrift on the other side of the hill, disintegrating on landing. Bond sets the self-destruct mechanism and they continue their escape across the Austrian border on Kara's cello case.

Bullet-proof glass

Hinged number plate

Rocket jet propulsion unit

Head-up display (as found in a cock-pit)

Laser beam cutter

Automatic missiles

Studded tyres

Automatically protruding skis for driving on ice

Some examples of the Aston Martin Volante's impressive array of armaments from The Living Daylights.

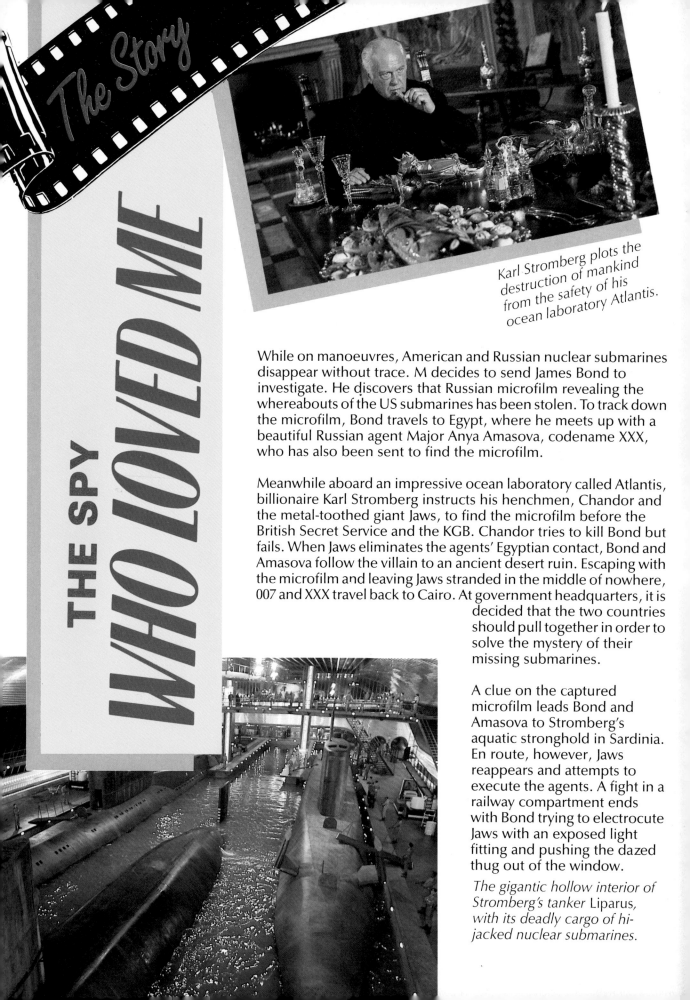

Karl Stromberg plots the destruction of mankind from the safety of his ocean laboratory Atlantis.

THE SPY
WHO LOVED ME

While on manoeuvres, American and Russian nuclear submarines disappear without trace. M decides to send James Bond to investigate. He discovers that Russian microfilm revealing the whereabouts of the US submarines has been stolen. To track down the microfilm, Bond travels to Egypt, where he meets up with a beautiful Russian agent Major Anya Amasova, codename XXX, who has also been sent to find the microfilm.

Meanwhile aboard an impressive ocean laboratory called Atlantis, billionaire Karl Stromberg instructs his henchmen, Chandor and the metal-toothed giant Jaws, to find the microfilm before the British Secret Service and the KGB. Chandor tries to kill Bond but fails. When Jaws eliminates the agents' Egyptian contact, Bond and Amasova follow the villain to an ancient desert ruin. Escaping with the microfilm and leaving Jaws stranded in the middle of nowhere, 007 and XXX travel back to Cairo. At government headquarters, it is decided that the two countries should pull together in order to solve the mystery of their missing submarines.

A clue on the captured microfilm leads Bond and Amasova to Stromberg's aquatic stronghold in Sardinia. En route, however, Jaws reappears and attempts to execute the agents. A fight in a railway compartment ends with Bond trying to electrocute Jaws with an exposed light fitting and pushing the dazed thug out of the window.

The gigantic hollow interior of Stromberg's tanker Liparus, *with its deadly cargo of hijacked nuclear submarines.*

The impressive sphinx of Egypt provides the backdrop for 007's investigations into some stolen microfilm.

Q arrives in Sardinia with the latest in sophisticated transport – a Lotus Esprit, fully equipped for any emergency. Pretending to be journalists, Bond and Amasova tour Atlantis and are intrigued by the scale model of a colossal oil tanker called the *Liparus*. Upon leaving Stromberg, Bond's Lotus is attacked by enemy gunfire. Putting the remarkable car through its paces, Bond outsmarts his adversaries and, converting the vehicle into a submersible, takes a closer look at Atlantis.

The terrifying Jaws tries to kill Bond by biting him in the neck with his steel teeth.

Boarding a nuclear submarine, Bond and Amasova study the *Liparus* before being swallowed by its gigantic hollow interior. Stromberg explains his plan to Bond – to destroy Moscow and New York with nuclear missiles. "Global destruction will follow," he proudly announces. "I intend to change the face of history by creating a world, a new and beautiful world below the sea. Today civilization is corrupt. Eventually it will destroy itself. I'm merely accelerating the process."

Amasova is taken by the madman to his underwater complex. Bond, meanwhile, engineers the escape of the imprisoned submarine crews. With only minutes to spare, he reprogrammes the nuclear missiles to destroy the submarines instead of Moscow and New York, sinking the tanker in a series of explosions. Instructed by the Pentagon to blow Stromberg and Atlantis out of the water, Bond has only a few hours to reach the base and rescue XXX.

In desperation, Stromberg tries to harpoon Bond but is shot dead. As torpedoes rip huge holes in the base, Bond avoids capture by Jaws by dropping him in a shark pen, using a magnet to lift him by his teeth. Together Bond and Amasova make their escape as Atlantis sinks below the waves.

VILLAINS' GALLERY

(Part Two)

ERNST STAVRO BLOFELD

One of James Bond's deadliest enemies was the devious and power-mad Ernst Stavro Blofeld, head of SPECTRE. The evil genius behind a number of sinister plans for world domination, his trademark was a beautiful white cat. Bond finally came face to face with the villain inside a rocket base within an extinct volcano. A cruel man with an ugly scar across his right cheek, Blofeld survived his ordeal with 007 and returned to menace him on two further assignments.

This clever mastermind altered his facial appearance by plastic surgery and managed to catch Bond off-guard. But he could not outwit Bond, as he discovered when he attempted to destroy military bases with the aid of a powerful laser satellite and 007 left him helplessly trapped in an escape pod

Blofeld, the head of SPECTRE, has been played by three actors, Donald Pleasence (illustrated), Telly Savalas and Charles Gray.

above the devasted remains of his secret oil rig headquarters.

MR WINT AND MR KYDD

Two of the most vicious villains Bond ever confronted were Mr Wint and Mr Kydd. Working as a team, these professional hoods were cold-bloodedly eliminating members of a diamond smuggling gang before their bizarre killing spree was cut short by James Bond's timely interference.

Diamond smugglers Mr Wint and Mr Kydd prepare to assassinate another innocent victim in Diamonds Are Forever.

DR KANANGA/MR BIG

Dr Kananga proves to be a particularly deadly opponent for Bond as he is also the powerful New York hoodlum and heroin smuggler Mr Big. It is here in a run-down area of Harlem that Bond comes face to face with Kananga for the first time. As Mr Big, he orders his henchmen to kill 007. Bond overpowers his assassins with the help of Felix Leiter and meets up with Kananga in the Caribbean island of San Monique where the villain doubles as the Prime Minister. Here he uses voodoo and superstition to protect his drug smuggling operation. In an exciting climax Kananga tries to kill Bond and the beautiful tarot-card reader Solitaire by feeding them to the sharks. They escape when Bond turns his watch – a Q invention – into a saw and uses it to cut them free. In a last fight, Bond forces a compressed air pellet into Kananga's mouth which expands until the evil doctor explodes with a bang.

Mr Big threatens Bond's life for interfering in his affairs while his evil henchman Tee Hee looks on in Live And Let Die.

BARON SAMEDI

Baron Samedi is Kananga's henchman in San Monique. Yet Samedi is no ordinary villain. He uses black magic and lethal snake venom to eliminate his victims during a strange voodoo ritual. Bond finds Samedi one of his strangest foes. Even by the end of the mission 007 cannot be sure that the Baron is really dead; his spectral figure appears – complete with eerie laugh – on the train in which Bond and Solitaire are travelling home together.

The elusive and rather sinister Baron Samedi who uses his supernatural powers to complete his master's diabolical plans.

Q's INVENTIONS

Bond demonstrates the remarkable capabilities of the ingenious wetbike.

As well as devising a whole range of impressive personal gadgets to aid 007 on vital life or death missions, Q's more sophisticated weaponry has included all manner of transport like the specially adapted Aston Martin DB5 and Volante and the Lotus Esprit. A high-speed motor-bike which rides on water, known as a wetbike, came in very handy when James Bond had to reach Karl Stromberg's ocean fortress Atlantis in a hurry. Having just prevented a plot to obliterate New York and Moscow, 007 skims the surface of the water in a race against time to rescue the kidnapped Russian agent Major Anya Amasova before the US Navy retaliates by blowing Atlantis out of the water.

Another close shave for Bond resulted from a frantic speed-boat chase through the canals of Venice. As his pursuers gain on him, Bond takes to dry land by revealing one of the many secrets of his high-speed gondola. At the press of a button, the narrow boat transforms into a hovercraft and, scattering pigeons left and

007's personal jet aircraft called the AcroStar stops off for refuelling in the opening sequence from Octopussy. It is only 3.5m (12ft) long with a 5m (17ft) wing span but can reach a top speed of 496 km/h (310mph).

right, glides gracefully across St Mark's Square past hundreds of surprised spectators.

Q's expertise at designing fast and efficient means for Bond to out-run the enemy was not restricted to land or sea based inventions. The brains behind the Secret Service's most ingenious devices was just as much at home in the air. His aerial contraptions have included the tiny but fast AcroStar that could be launched from the back of a horse box, a personal jet pack that enabled Bond to make a quick getaway from behind enemy lines and an amazing one-man autogyro affectionately referred to as Little Nellie.

Little Nellie helps Bond to search some volcanic craters in Japan. A formidable fleet of black SPECTRE helicopters gives chase, but not only is the lightweight plane able to out-manoeuvre and out-accelerate the enemy, Q has also equipped it with some devastating attachments: two machine-guns bolted to the front with a range of 100 metres, two forward-firing rocket launchers that spew death and destruction in the form of heat seeking air-to-air missiles and a flame gun that fires astern and is accompanied by two powerful smoke ejectors. An added bonus is the inclusion of aerial mines. The SPECTRE pilots have good reason to regret their confrontation with James Bond, 007.

"I never joke about my work," Q sternly reminds 007 on numerous occasions. For this, Bond is relieved. He knows that the department's gadgets, however bizarre or unusual, can mean the difference between life and death to a secret agent.

Q shows Bond how Little Nellie works in You Only Live Twice. This miniature helicopter has a top speed of 208 km/h (130mph).

Bond's Japanese colleagues are amazed by the compactness of Little Nellie. It weighs just 113kg (250lb) and was transported to Japan in four cases.

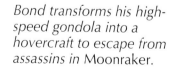

Bond transforms his high-speed gondola into a hovercraft to escape from assassins in Moonraker.

33

DICE WITH DEATH

START

Help James Bond escape with secret plans from

Dr No's Island. Throw a 6 to escape.

Interrogated by KGB. Go back 2 squares.

Transfer to plane. Move forward 3 squares.

Escape from Stromberg. Move forward 2 squares.

Shot down by Scaramanga's laser beam. Go back 3 squares.

Caught by Dr No's dragon. Miss a go

Rescue Honey Ryder. Move forward 1 square.

Car destroyed. Miss a go.

Transfer to power launch. Move forward 2 squares.

Captured by Goldfinger. Throw a 3 to escape.

Enemy agents chase boat. Go back 2 squares.

Drive Lotus Esprit. Move forward 4 squares.

Helicopter attacks. Go back 2 squares.

Lotus dives underwater. Go back 2 squares.

Boat turns into hovercraft. Move forward 2 squares.

Enemy cars appear. Miss a go.

Dr No's island to the safety of M's headquarters.

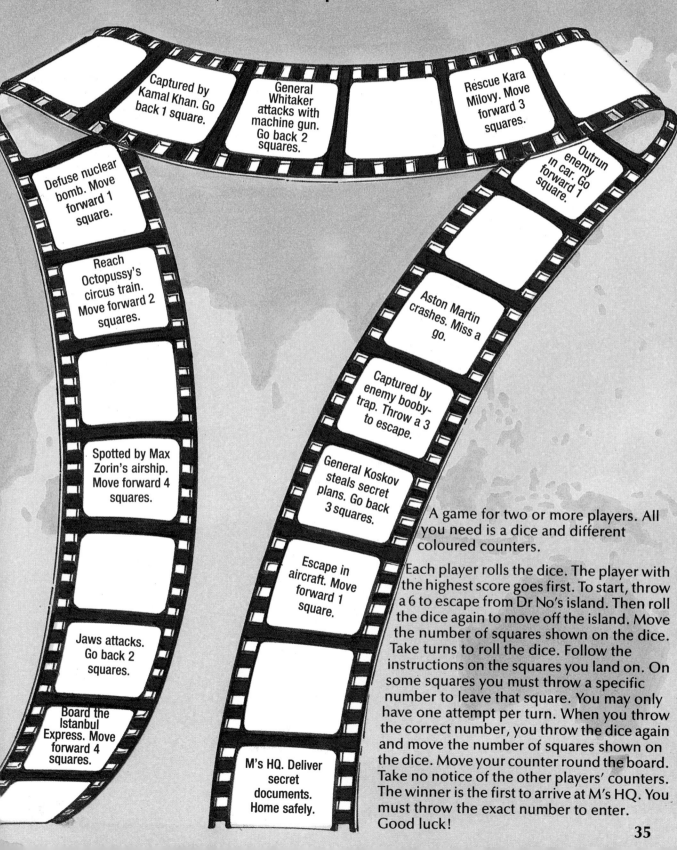

Captured by Kamal Khan. Go back 1 square.

General Whitaker attacks with machine gun. Go back 2 squares.

Rescue Kara Milovy. Move forward 3 squares.

Outrun enemy in car. Go forward 1 square.

Defuse nuclear bomb. Move forward 1 square.

Reach Octopussy's circus train. Move forward 2 squares.

Aston Martin crashes. Miss a go.

Spotted by Max Zorin's airship. Move forward 4 squares.

Captured by enemy booby-trap. Throw a 3 to escape.

General Koskov steals secret plans. Go back 3 squares.

Escape in aircraft. Move forward 1 square.

Jaws attacks. Go back 2 squares.

Board the Istanbul Express. Move forward 4 squares.

M's HQ. Deliver secret documents. Home safely.

A game for two or more players. All you need is a dice and different coloured counters.

Each player rolls the dice. The player with the highest score goes first. To start, throw a 6 to escape from Dr No's island. Then roll the dice again to move off the island. Move the number of squares shown on the dice. Take turns to roll the dice. Follow the instructions on the squares you land on. On some squares you must throw a specific number to leave that square. You may only have one attempt per turn. When you throw the correct number, you throw the dice again and move the number of squares shown on the dice. Move your counter round the board. Take no notice of the other players' counters. The winner is the first to arrive at M's HQ. You must throw the exact number to enter. Good luck!

THE SECRET WEAPONS

Blofeld's deadly rocket silo inside an extinct volcano in You Only Live Twice.

When faced with stopping an evil villain's plan to destroy the world, James Bond must first conquer all manner of sinister machines and deadly devices.

SPECTRE's chief, Ernst Stavro Blofeld, became one of 007's main adversaries due to his continual attempts to use sinister secret weapons to bring the world powers to their knees. When orbiting Russian and American space capsules disappear, Bond unearths a giant rocket designed to capture manned satellites within an enormous extinct volcano. But before the rocket can set off on its final mission to capture a Russian space capsule and bring the world to the brink of war, 007 infiltrates the hideout with the help of the Japanese Secret Service led

The diamond satellite under construction at Willard Whyte's space research station in Diamonds Are Forever.

by Tiger Tanaka and destroys the base by activating the lava flow beneath the crater floor.

When a large supply of diamonds goes missing from a mining company in South Africa, Bond once again finds Blofeld up to his old tricks. This time SPECTRE is using the precious stones to construct a fantastic orbiting laser weapon that can be targeted at the Superpowers' defence systems, everything from a missile silo in North Dakota to a nuclear submarine. Racing against time, Bond arrives at Blofeld's control centre to prevent him from directing his laser cannon at Washington DC.

Powerful lasers were also the weapons of Francisco Scaramanga. Using energy generated from the sun's rays, Scaramanga demonstrated the destructive capabilities of solex – a device which converts radiation from the sun into pure energy – by blowing up Bond's plane, stranding him on the evil mastermind's desert island.

Atlantis, Stromberg's impressive ocean labortory and headquarters.

Hijacked nuclear submarines played an important role in Karl Stromberg's plan to wipe out the human race. Trapping the submarines within the hollow interior of a 600,000-tonne supertanker called *Liparus*, Stromberg programmed their deadly

ballistic missiles to destroy New York and Moscow, while he sheltered in relative safety on the ocean floor within his fantastic science complex – Atlantis.

Even space could be doubly dangerous, as 007 discovered when, accompanied by CIA agent Dr Holly Goodhead, he took an unscheduled shuttle flight to the colossal hideout of megalomaniac Hugo Drax. Drax planned to annihilate all human life on earth with a deadly nerve gas created from the seeds of a rare jungle orchid. To stop him, Bond

Scaramanga uses his powerful laser to obliterate Bond's only means of escape in The Man With The Golden Gun.

Stromberg's supertanker, the Liparus, *swallowing a nuclear submarine in* The Spy Who Loved Me.

reveals the space station's whereabouts to a military fleet of American astronauts, by smashing the radar cloaking device.

An innocent-looking airship provided the secret headquarters of Max Zorin, a villain intent on destroying half the coast of California with a man-made earthquake. Bond found some unexpected assistance from Zorin's henchwoman May Day when she winched him out of an underground cavern full of high explosives on a crane carrying the deadly circular-shaped detonator.

The fantastic orbiting space station in Moonraker plays a vital part in Hugo Drax's plan for world domination.

Superior weaponry was the obsession of Brad Whitaker, a self-styled general who, with the help of a military defector, tricked the Russians into supplying weapons to their enemy, the Afghan freedom-fighters. Bond is forced to take on the armaments fanatic single-handed when he infiltrates his headquarters. This becomes a particularly dangerous assignment because Whitaker retaliates with a sophisticated super-rapid-fire machine-gun containing its own built-in bullet-proof shield.

007 successfully completes his assignment to stop Max Zorin blowing up Silicon Valley by destroying his airship in A View To A Kill.

Brad Whitaker attacks Bond with his super-rapid-fire machine gun in The Living Daylights.

007 usually finds out the hard way that it is not only the masterminds who threaten death and destruction with their lethal array of secret weapons. Goldfinger's personal assistant and chauffeur Oddjob, for example, was a Korean martial arts expert who made use of a special deadly black bowler hat. With a steel brim, it doubled as a terrifying projectile when expertly thrown.

Then there was Jaws, perhaps the most intimidating of all Bond's adversaries. A giant, over 2 metres (7 feet), his most destructive quality apart from his enormous strength, were the strange metal teeth that he used as a formidable weapon.

Dr Kananga's henchman Tee Hee proved to be a worthy opponent even for James Bond. He had some particularly nasty surprises up his sleeve as 007 discovered when he followed a mysterious voodoo cult and drug smuggling organization from New York to

Goldfinger's deadly henchman Oddjob hurls his steel-rimmed bowler hat at Bond to stop him defusing a neutron bomb inside Fort Knox.

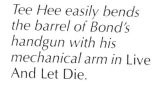

Tee Hee easily bends the barrel of Bond's handgun with his mechanical arm in Live And Let Die.

Jaws' metal teeth can bite through anything, including a wooden shelf, in The Spy Who Loved Me.

San Monique. Armed with an iron claw instead of a right hand, Tee Hee takes great delight in explaining to Bond how his entire arm was ripped off by one of Louisiana's less friendly inhabitants, the crocodile. Later, within the confines of a railway carriage, Bond and the metal-armed villain fight one last desperate battle.

Severing the operating cables in Tee Hee's metal arm, Bond locks the snapping claw on to a window ledge. With Tee Hee trapped and unable to escape, Bond seizes his chance and pushes the assassin through the train window.

MOONRAKER

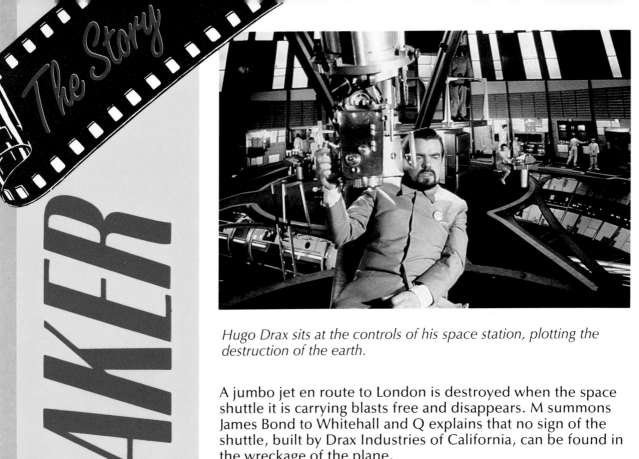

Hugo Drax sits at the controls of his space station, plotting the destruction of the earth.

A jumbo jet en route to London is destroyed when the space shuttle it is carrying blasts free and disappears. M summons James Bond to Whitehall and Q explains that no sign of the shuttle, built by Drax Industries of California, can be found in the wreckage of the plane.

On arrival in California, Bond is met by Corinne Dufour who flies him to the home of the Drax Corporation and research centre for the Moonraker shuttle programme. Drax's residence is a beautiful French palace brought from Europe, rebuilt in the American desert and surrounded by a floral oasis. A billionaire, Drax wanted to buy the Eiffel Tower but the authorities refused.

"Look after Mr Bond," Drax tells his henchman. "See that some harm comes to him." While looking around the space establishment, Bond meets Dr Holly Goodhead. She is very apologetic when a centrifuge device for simulating gravity goes out of control and nearly kills Bond. Drax tries to eliminate Bond the next day while they are out shooting, but fails.

Jaws holds Bond in a deadly grip as the two fight it out aboard a cable car.

Some stolen blueprints take Bond to Venice where he only escapes death by converting his gondola into a hovercraft and outrunning his adversaries. Bond breaks into a secret laboratory and steals a phial of colourless liquid which Q discovers is a nerve gas, lethal to humans but not animals.

It comes from a rare orchid and this lead takes Bond and Dr Holly Goodhead, whom Bond discovers is a CIA agent, to Brazil. There his old enemy Jaws tries to throw him from the roof of a cable car.

Escaping from the giant, Dr Holly Goodhead is captured by Drax's men. Meanwhile Bond travels up the Amazon in search of Drax's secret headquarters and is attacked by a number of enemy speed-boats. As a waterfall looms, Bond converts his boat into a hang-glider and floats away, while the unlucky Jaws and his cohorts plunge helplessly to the river-bed far below. On reaching Drax's hideout, Bond is thrown to a giant python which he manages to kill.

Bond watches as shuttles blast off into space. Drax orders Bond and Goodhead to be placed in the chamber below the rocket engines. Escaping, they board a shuttle and are surprised to see it is full of young people. After the shuttle leaves the earth's atmosphere, it docks at a vast orbiting space station. Drax explains how he plans to destroy mankind with the deadly nerve gas. "Here in the untainted cradle of the heavens will be created a new super race, a race of perfect physical specimens."

To stop the madman, Bond de-activates the radar jamming device that rendered the station invisible to earth scanners. American shuttles invade the complex and Drax's men are overpowered. Bond and Goodhead, with help from Jaws (who has fallen in love and reformed his character), blast off in one of the shuttles and intercept the nerve gas probes before they can contaminate earth.

A furious battle takes place aboard the space station as Bond races against time to prevent Drax from contaminating the earth's atmosphere with deadly nerve gas.

One of Drax's Moonraker space shuttles prepares for lift-off from his secret jungle hideout.

VILLAINS' GALLERY (Part Three)

FRANCISCO SCARAMANGA

Another of James Bond's enemies, almost as deadly as Blofeld, was Francisco Scaramanga. Known throughout the criminal fraternity as the world's highest paid assassin, his trademark was a golden gun with 23-carat gold bullets that he used on his unfortunate victims. To escape detection, the gun was cleverly assembled from seemingly innocent accessories including a cigarette case, a lighter, a cufflink and a pen.

A crackshot at the age of 15, Scaramanga was recruited by the KGB, but decided there was more money to be made as an independent killer.

Charging the phenomenal sum of $1 million for each assassination, this cool, suave villain turned an island paradise into his headquarters. Bond needed all his ingenuity to out-think and out-draw such a highly dangerous adversary.

The highest paid assassin in the world, the sinister Francisco Scaramanga, better known to his enemies as the man with the golden gun.

NICK NACK

Henchmen come in all shapes and sizes. From the towering metal-toothed giant Jaws to the 1.2 metre (3ft 10in) Nick Nack, Scaramanga's servant, bodyguard and heir. It was Nick Nack who controlled the deadly schemes dreamed up by his master in his various attempts to kill 007. Not until the very end of the assignment, after the defeat of the man with the golden gun, does Nick Nack get his come-uppance, when Bond locks him inside a conveniently sized suitcase.

Bond's smallest opponent, Nick Nack, was just as deadly as his master Scaramanga.

JAWS

2.3 metres (7ft 4in) tall, Jaws first appeared as the deadly assistant of the madman Karl Stromberg. While Stromberg was busy stealing nuclear submarines, James Bond was battling with the colossal henchman. The seemingly indestructible Jaws killed by means of his murderous metal teeth. His favourite method of killing was to bite into the victim's jugular vein. 007, whose strength was no match for this giant, had to rely on cunning to outwit him. After a vicious fight in a railway carriage, Bond tries to electrocute Jaws but his plan fails. Later, in Stromberg's ocean hideout, Atlantis, Bond uses a magnet to lift Jaws by the teeth and drop him into Stromberg's shark tank. But while Bond escapes and Atlantis blows up, Jaws sinks his teeth into the sharks and lives to fight again.

Much to Bond's surprise, Jaws reappears as a bodyguard and paid assassin for Hugo Drax, the French billionaire. Once again, Bond finds himself struggling for survival against the giant – this time on the roof of a Brazilian cable car as it sways back and forth halfway up a mountainside. Bond jumps to safety but Jaws crashes into the terminal below.

Fortunately Jaws falls in love and, during the explosive drama aboard Drax's orbiting space station, realizes the error of his ways in time to help 007 thwart the mastermind's plan for world domination.

The powerful Jaws demonstrates his superhuman strength when he threatens to crush Bond with a rock in The Spy Who Loved Me.

43

OCTOPUSSY

When a British Secret Service agent is found murdered in East Germany, two bizarre facts surround his death. Firstly, he is disguised as a circus clown and, secondly, he is clutching a fake of one of the priceless Fabergé eggs made for the Russian royal family by Carl Fabergé in 1897.

When a real Fabergé egg comes up for auction at Sotheby's, M sends Bond to investigate. He discovers that the jewel is now in the collection of an exiled Afghan prince called Kamal Khan. Following Khan to his home in Udaipur, 007 uncovers a gang of jewel thieves run by the glamorous Octopussy.

Kamal Khan, whose sinister plans for world domination include causing a nuclear accident.

Unbeknown to Bond, the priceless treasures smuggled into West Germany in Octopussy's circus troupe are stolen from the Russian vaults by the sinister General Orlov. While in India Bond confronts Khan who, concerned by the agent's interference in his plans, orders his henchman Gobinda to slay him. After an exciting chase through the market place in small electric taxi cabs, Bond manages to elude his enemies.

Eventually Bond is captured by Gobinda and taken to Khan's headquarters but he escapes. However, this leads to more danger when Khan organizes a tiger hunt with 007 as bait. Clambering aboard a tourist boat Bond outsmarts his pursuers and, inside a fake crocodile skin, makes his way to Octopussy's palace.

Khan is furious to find Bond alive on Octopussy's island. Although he wants her unharmed, he orders his thugs to invade the palace and kill Bond. The attack fails but Bond falls into the lake during the fight and Octopussy believes him to be dead.

Bond escapes from Gobinda's men in an electric taxi cab.

*Bond and Gobinda fight
to the death on the
fuselage of Khan's plane
in the film's exciting
climax.*

Later, in East Germany,
Bond watches as
Octopussy's circus train
is prepared for one of its
frequent trips to the
West. 007 is shocked to
discover something
aboard a carriage that is
far more sinister than
smuggled jewels.
General Orlov has
planted a nuclear bomb
timed to explode after
the circus arrives at the
US airforce base in
Feldstat. Confronting the
madman, Bond learns
that his plan is to make
the Europeans believe
that the detonated bomb
is an American accident,
thus forcing US troops
out of West Germany and
leaving the NATO
countries defenceless
against communist
invasion.

*007 races against time to defuse
the nuclear bomb Khan has
planted in a US airforce base in
West Germany.*

Disguised as a clown, Bond manages to infiltrate the circus and
defuse the bomb with just seconds to spare. General Orlov's
plot is uncovered and he is killed, but Khan and Gobinda
escape with Octopussy – who knew nothing of the bomb – as
their prisoner. Bond climbs on to the plane's fuselage, but has
to fight Khan's henchman before he can pull Octopussy to
safety as the plane and its villainous pilot plunge over the edge
of a cliff.

*Determined to kill Bond,
Khan leads a tiger hunt
through his palace
grounds with 007 as bait.*

THE C·H·A·S·E·

Bond pursues May Day in what is left of his taxi cab from A View To A Kill.

Pursuing a villain can be highly dangerous as James Bond knows only too well. On one of his most difficult assignments, he had to stop the evil genius Max Zorin from destroying Silicon Valley in California. After a contact is killed in Paris, Bond sets off in pursuit of Zorin's sinister henchwoman May Day. When she parachutes to safety from the top of the Eiffel Tower, Bond is forced to steal a taxi cab and follow her through the busy city streets. His car first loses its roof and then falls apart as 007 tries to avoid the streams of oncoming traffic. Skilfully steering the front section to the river's edge, Bond has to watch helplessly as May Day escapes in a waiting speedboat.

The waters of the Louisiana swampland were the location for one of 007's dramatic escapes by speedboat. Hotly pursued by Dr Kananga's henchmen, Bond performs some amazing stunts as he attempts to outwit his enemies.

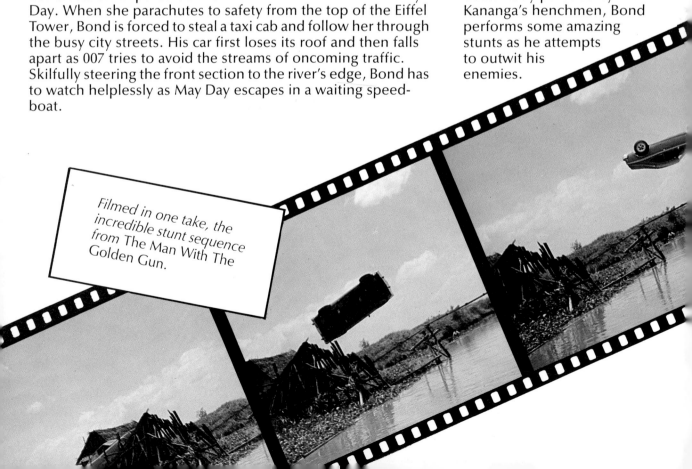

Filmed in one take, the incredible stunt sequence from The Man With The Golden Gun.

At one point he launches his boat through the air above the startled police. Unfortunately, the surprised police chief, Sheriff J. W. Pepper, accidently puts a bullet through the fuel tank, allowing Bond's enemies to close on him. Stealing another boat, Bond steers into a dock area and hides. Tricking his assailant, 007 sends the villain to a fiery death inside a ship's metal hold.

Another of Bond's chases teamed him up with the hysterical Sheriff Pepper when he tries to outrun Francisco Scaramanga's men. Driving an American Motors Hornet Hatchback, Bond is surprised to discover that the bridge over the river ahead has collapsed. Without flinching, he accelerates and catapults his car through the air, rolling a full 360 degrees, to land safely on the other side.

Bond's speed-boat, equipped with a 135 hp motor, leaps through the air above a startled Sheriff Pepper in Live And Let Die.

THE CHASE CONTINUED

Military manoeuvres on the Rock of Gibraltar involve Bond in a perilous assignment when an assassin starts killing the soldiers. Leaping on to the roof of the villain's Land Rover, it takes every bit of 007's skill and determination to keep a tight grip on the canvas covering, as the vehicle careers through the narrow streets. Bond manages to cut his way into the cab and overpower the driver, hurling the cargo of dynamite into the sea before it explodes.

While trailing the evil Kristatos, the man who planned to steal a top secret unit for ordering British submarines to fire their ballistic missiles, Bond encounters the beautiful Melina. Out to avenge the death of her parents, she and Bond are chased by international assassin Gonzales' henchmen. His Lotus Esprit blown up, Bond takes to the bumpy country roads in Melina's Citroën 2CV. Bouncing down mountainsides, leaping across the roofs of other vehicles, this amazing little car spectacularly saves its occupants from capture.

Another mission involved an escape in a strange moon buggy from Willard Whyte's space research establishment, in the Nevada desert, which had been taken over by Blofeld and his men. Crashing through the wall of a huge pressurized dome, 007 finds his unusual transport more than a match

Spectators stare in amazement as Bond dives through the roof of an assassin's Land Rover in The Living Daylights.

for the security vehicles and balloon-tyre lunar bikes sent out after him.

While investigating Dr Kananga's drugs empire, Bond and the mastermind's beautiful accomplice, Solitaire, take to the dusty highway in a refurbished London double-decker bus. Pursued by a team of assassins, Bond deliberately drives the bus under a low bridge. The roof comes

crashing down on top of the car behind, thus allowing them time to make their escape.

When SPECTRE's Ernst Stavro Blofeld orders his henchmen to kill Bond and the Japanese agent Kissy Suzuki, help comes from an unexpected quarter. As the assassins' car closes in on Bond and his companion, a huge helicopter descends

48

A camera crew captures on film James Bond's Lotus Esprit as it attempts to outrun an enemy helicopter from The Spy Who Loved Me.

As well as being an expert driver, Bond is also a skilled pilot. In one exciting chase, he has to outsmart a deadly heat-seeking missile in one of Q's most brilliant inventions – the AcroStar jet. Dodging and weaving to escape the rocket, Bond performs a daring stunt. He flies through the open hangar doors of his enemy's air-base followed by the missile and then speeds out of the hangar between the closing doors, leaving the missile trapped inside. The air-base is obliterated in a ball of flames as 007 pilots his tiny jet to safety.

from the sky. Tiger Tanaka, the head of the Japanese Secret Service, lowers a powerful electromagnet that picks up the enemy and drops them into the sea.

While on the trail of Willard Whyte's kidnappers, Bond is pursued through the streets of Las Vegas by the Nevada police department. Steering his girlfriend Tiffany's red Mustang into a narrow alley, Bond is horrified to see an exit half the width of the road. Throwing his weight to one side, 007 tips the car on to two wheels and, tyres squealing, escapes.

Bond tips his car on to two wheels to escape through a narrow alley in Diamonds Are Forever.

THE LIVING DAYLIGHTS

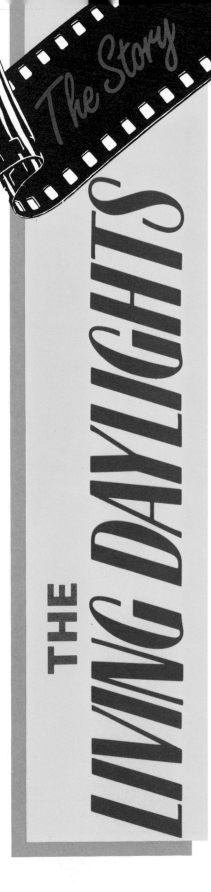

The beautiful cellist Kara Milovy whose love for General Koskov leads her into international espionage.

At a concert in Bratislava, Czechoslovakia, James Bond is instructed by the British Secret Service to protect KGB defector General Koskov from a suspected assassin and transport him safely to the West. Bond shoots at the would-be killer, but decides only to frighten his opponent when he realizes it is a beautiful girl whom he noticed playing in the orchestra.

With Q's help, Bond sneaks Koskov across the border by sending him through the trans-Siberian pipeline. Before Koskov can explain the full details of his investigations into a plot to kill top British and American agents, he is kidnapped from a secret hideout near London by a Russian agent. Bond is sent back to Czechoslovakia to rescue Koskov and, under instructions from M, to kill General Pushkin whom Koskov accused of being the brains behind the assassination attempt. For the trip, Q gives him a key-ring with a stun gas pellet that is activated by whistling and is packed with explosives.

Bond meets up with the cellist he witnessed shoot at Koskov. He discovers her name is Kara Milovy and that Koskov set up the attack himself. Suspecting the general of being a double agent, Bond lies to Milovy, who confesses her love for Koskov, and tells her that he is safe in England.

Koskov's henchman, Necros, tries to strangle Bond to stop him taking control of the plane with its deadly cargo of drugs.

With the secret police on their tail, Bond and Milovy escape to the mountains. Crossing the border into Austria proves hazardous, however, and Bond has to depend on his Aston Martin Volante's arsenal of secret weaponry to protect them.

Hearing that Bond is now in Austria, Koskov and his villainous sidekick Brad Whitaker plan to kill another agent and lay the blame at Pushkin's feet. Bond visits

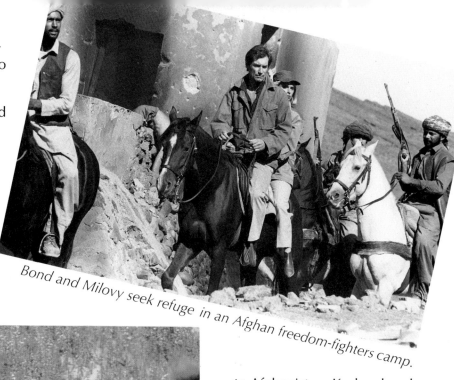

Bond and Milovy seek refuge in an Afghan freedom-fighters camp.

Skilfully steering his Aston Martin Volante across a frozen lake, Bond narrowly escapes a fiery death when a deadly tank shell explodes in his wake.

Bond's gunfire holds the Russians at bay so he can escape in Koskov's plane loaded with opium.

General Pushkin who claims innocence over the deaths of various foreign agents. Believing him to be telling the truth, 007 fakes an assassination so that Koskov will think Bond has carried out M's instructions.

Together Bond and Kara Milovy follow Koskov to Tangier, but both are kidnapped and flown

to Afghanistan. Koskov hands Bond over to the communist authorities for killing General Pushkin and accuses Kara of being an accomplice to the crime. Bond and Kilovy escape when 007 activates the key-ring's gas pellet and overpowers the guards.

They join a band of Afghan rebels and Bond discovers that Koskov is selling arms to them and receiving supplies of opium as part of the deal. Hiding aboard Koskov's plane, Bond kills the villain's henchman Necros by throwing him out of the plane, together with the opium. Then the plane swoops down on the rebels' camp and Bond destroys an advancing Russian task force.

Bond enters Whitaker's apartment and informs him that the opium is lost. Furious, the tough arms-dealer tries to kill 007 with some of the sophisticated weapons that he sells to the highest bidder. But Bond's exploding key-ring puts an end to this ruthless criminal. Koskov appears, but before he can kill Bond he is captured by Pushkin and sent back to Russia.

Sean Connery

BOND ACTORS

In the first films based on Ian Fleming's highly successful series of books, Sean Connery played James Bond. Connery gave the role his own distinctive style. He played him as a tough, likeable rogue who completed his various assignments with ruthless efficiency. Connery's adventures included the defeat of Dr No and his missile "toppling" device, retrieving a valuable cypher machine before it fell into the hands of enemy agents in *From Russia With Love* and foiling Goldfinger's sensational plot to explode an atomic device inside Fort Knox. In *Thunderball*, he stopped Emilio Largo from detonating a nuclear bomb and twice he faced Blofeld's sinister villainy in *You Only Live Twice* and *Diamonds Are Forever*.

Tim Dalton

Licence To Kill is the second James Bond film produced by Albert ("Cubby") Broccoli to feature Timothy Dalton in the title role. An actor with a great love for the theatre, Dalton starred in a number of films before taking over the reins of secret agent 007 from Roger Moore in 1987. His first adventure, *The Living Daylights*, concerned the attempts being made on the lives of top British and American agents by the Soviet defector, KGB General Koskov. Bond's assignments seem more dangerous with each new escapade, but Timothy Dalton is more than a match for the villains in his portrayal of 007.

Roger Moore

Roger Moore starred as James Bond from 1973 until 1986 but he was originally considered for the part when producers Broccoli and Harry Saltzman were casting for an actor to play 007 in the first Bond film, Dr No, in 1962. Commitment to the television series The Saint prevented Moore from auditioning. As 007, Roger Moore brought a more sauve and tongue-in-cheek attitude to the character, and his stint as the world's most famous secret agent included the series' most bizarre and surreal assignments. Live And Let Die, for example, offered a heady mixture of voodoo, superstition and drugs, while The Man With The Golden Gun pitted good against the evil of Scaramanga. A sprawling underwater city and a supertanker that swallowed submarines provided the ornate setting for The Spy Who Loved Me. In Moonraker, an orbiting space station endangered the human race, and stolen equipment of an extremely sensitive nature was the cause for concern in For Your Eyes Only. Octopussy centred around a plot to devastate a West German military base, and an underground mine full of high explosives posed a threat to America's Silicon Valley in A View To A Kill.

George Lazenby

George Lazenby was the second actor to play Bond but he only appeared in one film. On Her Majesty's Secret Service dealt out more treachery in the guise of the sinister Blofeld. Lazenby injected an intriguing aspect into 007's character which helped to bridge the gap between the very different acting talents of Sean Connery and Roger Moore.

Bond and his bride, Teresa, Contessa di Vicenzo.

VILLAINS' GALLERY
(Part Four)

MAX ZORIN

Bond finds himself up against a worthy adversary when he meets Max Zorin, a wealthy French industrialist. Zorin is highly respected by foreign governments, including Britain, but hides his truly evil nature until Bond uncovers a plot to destroy Silicon Valley – the home of the man-made microchip – in California with a man-made earthquake caused by detonating millions of tonnes of high explosive.

A cold and calculating killer, the psychopathic Zorin was actually born in Germany and became part of a Nazi experiment in genetics to create the ultimate human being. Having fled to the West, he set up his own company, Zorin Industries, with the intention of cornering the technological market. When Bond stops his plans to devastate the West Coast, Zorin kidnaps beautiful Stacey Sutton. To rescue her, Bond must defeat Zorin in a final showdown on top of one of the main support towers of San Francisco's famous Golden Gate Bridge.

Two of Bond's deadliest foes: the ruthless Max Zorin who is bent on cornering the world microchip market and his accomplice May Day from A View To A Kill.

MAY DAY

Zorin's lover and bodyguard is the delectable, but deadly, May Day. In a dramatic chase through the steel framework of the Eiffel Tower, May Day demonstrates her cold courage by leaping to safety. A professional killer, May Day assassinates Bond's contacts including French undercover agent Monsieur Aubergine and friend of the Secret Service Sir Godfrey Tibbett. Also the result of a genetic experiment, May Day is as evil as her master, but changes sides when Zorin double-crosses her. She helps Bond to divert the detonator from its target – a disused silver mine that Zorin has packed with explosives – and saves Silicon Valley. However, in doing so, she blows herself up.

FRANZ SANCHEZ

Franz Sanchez is 007's latest and, perhaps, most dangerous opponent. A billionaire, Sanchez has accumulated his incredible wealth through his position as one of the world's most notorious drug barons. He leaves the safety of Central America, where he has the protection of bribed politicians, for the Bahamas to snatch back his girlfriend who has run off with one of his lieutenants. There Sanchez is captured by Bond and Felix Leiter, but is later freed by his accomplices and takes his revenge on the unsuspecting Leiter. Although the British Secret Service would prefer to let the Americans bring the villain to justice, Bond disagrees and, against M's wishes, sets out to even the score.

Drugs baron Franz Sanchez proves to be one of Bond's most dangerous opponents in Licence To Kill.

MILTON KREST

Sanchez surrounds himself with a veritable army of henchmen and paid assassins, none of whom is more deadly than Milton Krest. Krest runs a distribution base for Sanchez's drug-smuggling operation and helps Sanchez to escape from jail. His secret laboratory is concealed aboard a marine research vessel called the *Wavekrest*. Together with cohorts Truman-Lodge, Dario and Colonel Heller, Sanchez and Krest form a truly formidable force for James Bond to defeat.

Milton Krest, one of Sanchez's evil associates.

LICENCE TO KILL

Much to his fiancée's surprise, Felix Leiter accompanied by his best man James Bond arrives at his wedding by parachute.

When Franz Sanchez, an extremely wealthy drugs baron, is sighted in the Bahamas, the Drug Enforcement Administration plans to arrest him. Agent Felix Leiter is on the way to his wedding when he hears this news but joins them to catch the villain. He is accompanied on this highly dangerous, last-minute operation by his best man, none other than friend and colleague, James Bond. An exciting air chase takes place. Bond is lowered from his helicopter on to Sanchez's plane and captures him. Mission accomplished, the latecomers arrive at the church by parachuting down over the heads of the surprised wedding guests.

So the latest James Bond film, *Licence To Kill,* begins with the traditional spectacular pre-title sequence. Filming began on 18 July 1988 at the Churubusco Studios in Mexico City. Film locations outside Mexico City included Acapulco, Mexicali and Florida's Key West.

It was at Key West that one particular action sequence was shot. Milton Krest, Sanchez's criminal accomplice, decides not to let Sanchez rot in prison. As the heavily armoured security truck transports Sanchez to jail, it is attacked by his crooked cohorts. To add excitement to the scene, it was written into the script that the truck would plunge off a bridge into the ocean.

The film's second unit were responsible for setting up the stunts, which have to be meticulously planned. A special platform was constructed so the action inside the truck could be viewed as it sped along. Rehearsing the scene prior to filming meant driving the truck to the point where it would career out of control and crash through the safety barrier beside the road. Confident that the stunt would work, three cameras were set up to record the action. For the actual moment that the vehicle fell into the water a remote-controlled version was used.

Milton Krest's clever escape plan results in the drugs baron Sanchez being rescued while the truck transporting him to jail plummets into the ocean.

Free from captivity, Sanchez seeks revenge on Leiter and lowers the unfortunate agent into a shark pen. When Bond finds his friend with a note pinned to him saying "He disagreed with something that ate him," he is determined to bring Sanchez to justice whatever the cost. M revokes 007's licence to kill, demanding that he keep out of American affairs, but Bond's mind is made up. He enlists the help of one of Leiter's contacts, Pam Bouvier, and together they fly to Isthmus City, to Sanchez's casino. 007 cleverly infiltrates Sanchez's organization and wins the villain's approval. Against M's wishes, Q joins Bond to help out with his usual briefcase of gadgets including a sophisticated rifle which packs away to resemble an innocent camera.

Secured by a line from the helicopter, Bond clings to the tail fin of his adversary's aircraft.

An exciting chase on a mountain road ends with the tankers containing millions of pounds of narcotics exploding in a giant fireball.

THE MAKING OF / LICENCE TO KILL

Sanchez shows Bond a deadly cargo of narcotics en route from a top secret laboratory to a nearby port. It is here on a barren mountain road outside Mexicali in Mexico that the climax of *Licence To Kill* takes place. As the tankers containing the drugs set off across the hostile landscape, Bond and Pam follow in a crop-dusting plane. Bond lowers himself on to the roof of one of the moving trucks from the plane flying above and defeats Sanchez in a fight to the death.

To record every exciting moment of this dangerous stunt, a camera crew were mounted on top of the truck. The area to film the sequence was chosen by John Glen, making his fifth Bond film as director. The the crew had to contend with some harsh working conditions. The desert sands baked under the sun's relentless heat as temperatures soared well over 48°C (120°F). Again the film's second unit co-ordinated all the action scenes. They first had to build their own roads, clear away rocks and shrubs, level the ground and make artificial boulders from fibreglass.

Behind the scenes, the stars were the special effects team led by John Richardson. It is up to them to make all the explosions and crashes look as authentic as possible. One of the most

The situation looks decidedly grim for 007 when he finds himself at the mercy of the evil Sanchez.

James Bond's only hope of catching the enemy is by lowering himself from a crop-spraying plane onto the roof of the escaping truck.

spectacular stunts in *Licence To Kill* is a thrilling chase along a perilous mountain road in which five tankers crash into one another and explode.

The tankers were designed by the Kenworth Truck Company and driven by a team of stunt drivers. Remy Julienne, who supervized the driving, discussed the modifications to the vehicles with the company engineers at their factory in Seattle. These modifications included fitting one truck with a remote control unit and substituting wood for metal containers on

Determined to take revenge, Sanchez instructs his henchmen to lower the helpless Felix into a shark-infested tank.

Helicopters are used by the camera crew to film aerial stunt scenes.

others. One truck was especially designed to be driven tilted on its side.

Special care must be taken with explosions to avoid serious injury or accident. For the sequence in which one of the trucks disintegrates in a fireball, 2,300 litres (500 gallons) of petrol and a cocktail of explosives including gunpowder were used. What might seem to the audience, however, as one gigantic explosion, is in fact comprised of a number of smaller detonations, each perfectly synchronized to give a breathtaking overall effect.

For the actors, stunt men, film crews and director, shooting a James Bond film can be a long and, at times, arduous business. But as *Licence To Kill* proves, when it is all put together, their determination and professionalism add up to the best in big screen entertainment.

For filming close-ups of Bond on top of a moving tanker, the camera crew construct a special platform.

BOND QUIZ 2

FILMS:

1. What is the nickname of Albert R. Broccoli – the producer of the Bond films?

   Cubby

   Chubby   Tee Hee

                   Brad   Secret

                                     Fleming

2. How many people around the world have seen a Bond film?

   2 million

              98 million

                       2 billion

3. Pair the singer or group with the title song.

   1 Thunderball
   2 Live And Let Die   A a-ha
   3 The Spy Who Loved Me   B Shirley Bassey
   4 The Living Daylights   C Paul McCartney and Wings
   5 Diamonds Are Forever   D Tom Jones
                               E Carly Simon

4. These five James Bond films have been written using a cipher. What are they?

   A. S NAWO LG S CADD
   B. XJGE JMKKAS OALZ DGNW
   C. XGJ QGMJ WQWK GFDQ
   D. LZW KHQ OZG DGNWV EW
   E. YGDVXAFYWJ

1. How did Jaws and Dolly meet in the film *Moonraker*?

2. In which film does Bond make his escape in a moon buggy?

VILLAINS

1. Match the villain with the actor who played him or her.

   1 May Day   A Christopher Lee
   2 Jaws   B Harold Sakata
   3 Emilio Largo   C Lotte Lenya
   4 Oddjob   D Grace Jones
   5 Francisco Scaramanga   E Richard Kiel
   6 Rosa Klebb   F Adolfo Celi

2. Which of these villains had a mechanical claw instead of a hand?

                                           Tee Hee
   Jaws   Dr Kananga   May Day
                   Hugo Drax
   Oddjob

3. Who did SPECTRE agent Rosa Klebb send to kill Bond in *From Russia With Love*?

4. Which of the following villains survived their encounters with 007?

   Scaramanga   General Koskov   Mr Kydd
                   Goldfinger   Brad Whitaker
   Jaws   Red Grant   Kamal Khan
   Dr No

GADGETS

1. Which of the following gadgets are not found on James Bond's Aston Martin DB5?

machine guns   parachute   tyre slashers

skis   laser beam   rocket propulsion unit

flame thrower   radar

ejector seat   missile launcher

2. Which of these films did not feature a laser?

Diamonds Are Forever   *Moonraker*

Goldfinger   *From Russia With Love*

The Man With The Golden Gun

3. Q designed a vast array of fantastic gadgets to help Bond on an assignment. Which of the following were not designed by Q?

space shuttle   exploding radio

AcroStar jet   a bullet-firing ski stick

Lotus Esprit

solex laser gun   an acid-filled fountain pen

magnetic watch

3. In which film did this strange car/plane appear?

JAMES BOND

1. Which actor only played James Bond once?

2. Before becoming a secret agent, in which of the armed services did James Bond obtain the rank of commander?
the navy, the army, the air force, the SAS

3. James Bond's exploits have taken him into many dangerous locations. Which of these places hasn't he been to?

Brazil   France   Australia

India   The Moon   England

California   Istanbul   China

4. What was the name of James Bond's wife?

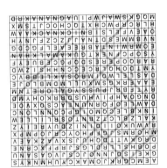

ANSWERS TO WORD PUZZLE

Answers to Bond Quiz 1 on page 22

Picture puzzle: Dr No, Goldfinger, Jaws, Max Zorin, Nick Nack.

Photograph: Trick question! The crocodile was quite harmless as it was a disguise used by Bond to infiltrate the defences of Octopussy's Indian palace.

Answers to Bond Quiz 2

Photographs

1. After Bond and Jaws fought on the roof of the cable car, Dolly rescued Jaws from the wreckage in *Moonraker*.

2. Bond used the moon buggy to escape from Willard Whyte's space research centre in *Diamonds Are Forever*.

3. The car belonged to Francisco Scaramanaga and at the flick of a switch became an aeroplane in *The Man With The Golden Gun*.

Gadgets

1. skis, flame thrower, laser beam, rocket propulsion unit, missile launcher. 2. *From Russia With Love*. 3. space shuttle, solex laser gun, exploding radio.

James Bond

1. George Lazenby. 2. The navy. 3. The Moon, Australia, China. 4. Teresa, Contessa di Vicenzo, but she called herself Tracy.

Villains

1. 1D, 2E, 3F, 4B, 5A, 6C. 2. Tee Hee. 3. Red Grant. 4. Jaws, General Koskov.

Films

1. Cubby 2. 2 billion 3. 1D, 2C, 3F, 4A, 5B. 4. The real letters of the alphabet were substituted by an alphabet beginning with the letter S, i.e. the letter A = S in the cipher, B = T, C = U etc. The films were: A. *A View To A Kill*. B. *From Russia With Love*. C. *For Your Eyes Only*. D. *The Spy Who Loved Me*. E. *Goldfinger*.

61